DEDICATION

This book is dedicated to all the amazing Cruisers out there who just wanna say SEA YA! for a bit...

YOU are my inspiration for producing this SEA YA! Cruise Planner and I'm honored to be a part of keeping all of your essential trip details organized! Have a fun and safe trip!

HOW TO USE

The purpose of this SEA YA! Cruise Planner is to keep all your various cruise trip plans & activities organized in one easy to find spot. Here are the available sections you can use to stay organized and effortlessly enjoy your trip!

1. Deposit tracker to help you plan and save money for your trip
2. Cruise countdown calendar
3. Flight information
4. Included 3 page cruise packing checklist
5. Cruise port and excursion planner
6. Activity planner
7. Cruise Itinerary
8. A lined cruise journal pages for recording memories!

THIS CRUISE JOURNAL BELONGS TO:

CRUISE SAVINGS

WE'RE SAVING FOR:

AMOUNT NEEDED: $

OUR GOAL DATE:

DEPOSIT TRACKER

AMOUNT DEPOSITED: **DATE DEPOSITED:**

$
$
$
$
$
$
$
$
$
$

CRUISE SAVINGS

DEPOSIT TRACKER

AMOUNT DEPOSITED: **DATE DEPOSITED:**

$ _____ _____

$ _____ _____

$ _____ _____

$ _____ _____

$ _____ _____

$ _____ _____

$ _____ _____

$ _____ _____

$ _____ _____

$ _____ _____

$ _____ _____

$ _____ _____

$ _____ _____

CRUISE DETAILS

NOTES

TO DO:

CRUISE DETAILS & REMINDERS:

CRUISE COUNTDOWN

MONTH: _____ **YEAR:** _____

M	T	W	T	F	S	S

FLIGHT INFORMATION

DATE: _____ DESTINATION: _____

AIRLINE:	
BOOKING NUMBER:	
DEPARTURE DATE:	
BOARDING TIME:	
GATE NUMBER:	
SEAT NUMBER:	
ARRIVAL / LANDING TIME:	

DATE: _____ DESTINATION: _____

AIRLINE:	
BOOKING NUMBER:	
DEPARTURE DATE:	
BOARDING TIME:	
GATE NUMBER:	
SEAT NUMBER:	
ARRIVAL / LANDING TIME:	

CRUISE PACKING CHECKLIST

CLOTHING	✓	ESSENTIALS	✓

CRUISE PACKING CHECKLIST

CLOTHING FOR HER	✓	CLOTHING FOR HIM	✓

ESSENTIALS	✓	FOR THE JOURNEY	✓

		IMPORTANT DOCUMENTS	✓

CRUISE PACKING CHECKLIST

CLOTHING FOR HER	✓	CLOTHING FOR HIM	✓
T-Shirts &, Tank Tops & Blouses		T-Shirts & Tank Tops	
Sundresses		Shorts	
Flip Flops, Sandals & Heels		Swim Wear	
Shorts & Pants		Jeans, Khakis	
Swimsuit & Cover Up		Formal Attire (dress shirt, shoes, etc.)	
T-Shirts &, Tank Tops & Blouses		Belt	
Aqua/Swimming Shoes		Tie	
Bras, Panties & Socks		Sandals / Sneakers	
Sunhat		Visor, Baseball Cap	
Sunglasses		T-Shirts &, Tank Tops & Blouses	
Formal Attire		Sunglasses	
Jewelry		Socks & Underwear	
ESSENTIALS	✓	**FOR THE JOURNEY**	✓
Lanyard		Carry On Bag	
Suntan Lotion		Cash / Local Currency	
Medication (motion sickness, etc.)		Credit Cards	
Travel Mug / Water Bottle		Phone Charger	
		Backpack	
		IMPORTANT DOCUMENTS	✓
		Passport & ID	
		Cruise Documents & Boarding Pass	
		Flight Information	

CRUISE EXCURSION PLANNER

ACTIVITY / EXCURSION OVERVIEW:

EST COST OF EXCURSION:

INCLUSIONS: ✓	**EXCLUSIONS:** ✓
FOOD & DRINK: ☐	☐
TRANSPORTATION: ☐	☐
GRATUITY: ☐	☐

ACTUAL COST:

IMPORTANT INFORMATION:

CONTACT: PHONE #:

MEET UP TIME: WHAT TO BRING:

ADDRESS:

CRUISE PORT PLANNER

DESTINATION: **DATE:**

THINGS TO DO / SEE:

- [ ]
- [ ]
- [ ]
- [ ]
- [ ]
- [ ]
- [ ]

WHERE TO EAT:

- [ ]
- [ ]
- [ ]
- [ ]
- [ ]
- [ ]
- [ ]

TRANSPORTATION DETAILS:

- [ ]
- [ ]
- [ ]
- [ ]
- [ ]

OTHER INFORMATION:

- [ ]
- [ ]
- [ ]
- [ ]
- [ ]

RETURN TO SHIP BY:

ALL ABOARD!

PRE-CRUISE TO DO LIST & CHECKLIST

1 MONTH BEFORE

2 WEEKS BEFORE

1 WEEK BEFORE

2 DAYS BEFORE

24 HOURS BEFORE

DAY OF TRAVEL

CRUISE PLANNER

WEEK OF:

MONDAY	TUESDAY	WEDNESDAY	THURSDAY
TO DO	TO DO	TO DO	TO DO
MEALS	MEALS	MEALS	MEALS

FRIDAY	SATURDAY	SUNDAY	NOTES
TO DO	TO DO	TO DO	
MEALS	MEALS	MEALS	MEALS

CRUISING TO DO LIST

CRUISE BUCKET LIST

PLACES I WANT TO VISIT:

_____
_____
_____
_____
_____
_____
_____
_____
_____
_____
_____
_____
_____
_____

THINGS I WANT TO SEE:

_____
_____
_____
_____
_____
_____
_____
_____
_____
_____
_____
_____
_____
_____
_____
_____
_____

TOP 3 DESTINATIONS:

_____
_____
_____

CRUISE ITINERARY

Monday

Tuesday

Wednesday

thursday

Friday

Saturday

Sunday

CRUISE OVERVIEW

MONTH:

MONDAY	TUESDAY	WEDNESDAY	THURSDAY	FRIDAY	SATURDAY	SUNDAY

CRUISE ACTIVITIES

WEEKLY ACTIVITY TRACKER: M T W T F S S

DAILY ACTIVITY PLANNER

DAILY ITINERARY

ACTIVITY: _____

TIME: _____

LOCATION: _____

WEATHER: ☀️ ⛅ 🌦️ ☁️ ⛈️

MEAL PLANNER

DAILY EXPENSES

TOTAL COST: _____

TOP ACTIVITIES

TIME: SCHEDULE:

NOTES:

CRUISE FRIENDS

FRIENDS ARE FOREVER

NAME:

PHONE NUMBER:

ADDRESS:

CABIN #:

FRIENDS ARE FOREVER

NAME:

PHONE NUMBER:

ADDRESS:

CABIN #:

FRIENDS ARE FOREVER

NAME:

PHONE NUMBER:

ADDRESS:

CABIN #:

FRIENDS ARE FOREVER

NAME:

PHONE NUMBER:

ADDRESS:

CABIN #:

There's Nothing Like Cruising Life!

CRUISE FRIENDS

FRIENDS ARE FOREVER

NAME:

PHONE NUMBER:

ADDRESS:

CABIN #:

FRIENDS ARE FOREVER

NAME:

PHONE NUMBER:

ADDRESS:

CABIN #:

FRIENDS ARE FOREVER

NAME:

PHONE NUMBER:

ADDRESS:

CABIN #:

FRIENDS ARE FOREVER

NAME:

PHONE NUMBER:

ADDRESS:

CABIN #:

There's Nothing Like Cruising Life!

CRUISE FRIENDS

FRIENDS ARE FOREVER

NAME:

PHONE NUMBER:

ADDRESS:

CABIN #:

FRIENDS ARE FOREVER

NAME:

PHONE NUMBER:

ADDRESS:

CABIN #:

FRIENDS ARE FOREVER

NAME:

PHONE NUMBER:

ADDRESS:

CABIN #:

FRIENDS ARE FOREVER

NAME:

PHONE NUMBER:

ADDRESS:

CABIN #:

There's Nothing Like Cruising Life!

CRUISE FRIENDS

FRIENDS ARE FOREVER

NAME:
PHONE NUMBER:
ADDRESS:
CABIN #:

FRIENDS ARE FOREVER

NAME:
PHONE NUMBER:
ADDRESS:
CABIN #:

FRIENDS ARE FOREVER

NAME:
PHONE NUMBER:
ADDRESS:
CABIN #:

FRIENDS ARE FOREVER

NAME:
PHONE NUMBER:
ADDRESS:
CABIN #:

There's Nothing Like Cruising Life!

CRUISE FRIENDS

FRIENDS ARE FOREVER

NAME:
PHONE NUMBER:
ADDRESS:
CABIN #:

FRIENDS ARE FOREVER

NAME:
PHONE NUMBER:
ADDRESS:
CABIN #:

FRIENDS ARE FOREVER

NAME:
PHONE NUMBER:
ADDRESS:
CABIN #:

FRIENDS ARE FOREVER

NAME:
PHONE NUMBER:
ADDRESS:
CABIN #:

There's Nothing Like Cruising Life!

CRUISE FRIENDS

FRIENDS ARE FOREVER

NAME:

PHONE NUMBER:

ADDRESS:

CABIN #:

FRIENDS ARE FOREVER

NAME:

PHONE NUMBER:

ADDRESS:

CABIN #:

FRIENDS ARE FOREVER

NAME:

PHONE NUMBER:

ADDRESS:

CABIN #:

FRIENDS ARE FOREVER

NAME:

PHONE NUMBER:

ADDRESS:

CABIN #:

There's Nothing Like Cruising Life!

MY CRUISE AGENDA

MY CRUISE AGENDA

MY CRUISE AGENDA

MY CRUISE AGENDA

MY CRUISE JOURNAL

DATE:

What I Did Today:

Highlight of the Day:

Thoughts & Reflections:

CRUISE SAVINGS

WE'RE SAVING FOR:

AMOUNT NEEDED:

OUR GOAL DATE:

$

DEPOSIT TRACKER

AMOUNT DEPOSITED: **DATE DEPOSITED:**

$

$

$

$

$

$

$

$

$

CRUISE SAVINGS

DEPOSIT TRACKER

AMOUNT DEPOSITED: **DATE DEPOSITED:**

$ _____

$ _____

$ _____

$ _____

$ _____

$ _____

$ _____

$ _____

$ _____

$ _____

$ _____

$ _____

$ _____

CRUISE DETAILS

NOTES

TO DO:

CRUISE DETAILS & REMINDERS:

CRUISE COUNTDOWN

MONTH: _____ **YEAR:** _____

M	T	W	T	F	S	S

FLIGHT INFORMATION

DATE: _____ DESTINATION: _____

AIRLINE:	
BOOKING NUMBER:	
DEPARTURE DATE:	
BOARDING TIME:	
GATE NUMBER:	
SEAT NUMBER:	
ARRIVAL / LANDING TIME:	

DATE: _____ DESTINATION: _____

AIRLINE:	
BOOKING NUMBER:	
DEPARTURE DATE:	
BOARDING TIME:	
GATE NUMBER:	
SEAT NUMBER:	
ARRIVAL / LANDING TIME:	

CRUISE PACKING CHECKLIST

CLOTHING	✓	ESSENTIALS	✓

CRUISE PACKING CHECKLIST

CLOTHING FOR HER	✓	CLOTHING FOR HIM	✓

ESSENTIALS	✓	FOR THE JOURNEY	✓

		IMPORTANT DOCUMENTS	✓

CRUISE PACKING CHECKLIST

CLOTHING FOR HER	✓	CLOTHING FOR HIM	✓
T-Shirts &, Tank Tops & Blouses		T-Shirts & Tank Tops	
Sundresses		Shorts	
Flip Flops, Sandals & Heels		Swim Wear	
Shorts & Pants		Jeans, Khakis	
Swimsuit & Cover Up		Formal Attire (dress shirt, shoes, etc.)	
T-Shirts &, Tank Tops & Blouses		Belt	
Aqua/Swimming Shoes		Tie	
Bras, Panties & Socks		Sandals / Sneakers	
Sunhat		Visor, Baseball Cap	
Sunglasses		T-Shirts &, Tank Tops & Blouses	
Formal Attire		Sunglasses	
Jewelry		Socks & Underwear	
ESSENTIALS	✓	**FOR THE JOURNEY**	✓
Lanyard		Carry On Bag	
Suntan Lotion		Cash / Local Currency	
Medication (motion sickness, etc.)		Credit Cards	
Travel Mug / Water Bottle		Phone Charger	
		Backpack	
		IMPORTANT DOCUMENTS	✓
		Passport & ID	
		Cruise Documents & Boarding Pass	
		Flight Information	

CRUISE EXCURSION PLANNER

ACTIVITY / EXCURSION OVERVIEW:

EST COST OF EXCURSION:

INCLUSIONS: ✓	**EXCLUSIONS:** ✓
FOOD & DRINK: ☐	☐
TRANSPORTATION: ☐	☐
GRATUITY: ☐	☐

ACTUAL COST:

IMPORTANT INFORMATION:

CONTACT: PHONE #:

MEET UP TIME: WHAT TO BRING:

ADDRESS:

CRUISE PORT PLANNER

DESTINATION: DATE:

THINGS TO DO / SEE:

- ☐
- ☐
- ☐
- ☐
- ☐
- ☐
- ☐

WHERE TO EAT:

- ☐
- ☐
- ☐
- ☐
- ☐
- ☐
- ☐

TRANSPORTATION DETAILS:

- ☐
- ☐
- ☐
- ☐
- ☐

OTHER INFORMATION:

- ☐
- ☐
- ☐
- ☐
- ☐

RETURN TO SHIP BY:

ALL ABOARD!

PRE-CRUISE TO DO LIST & CHECKLIST

1 MONTH BEFORE

2 WEEKS BEFORE

1 WEEK BEFORE

2 DAYS BEFORE

24 HOURS BEFORE

DAY OF TRAVEL

CRUISE PLANNER

WEEK OF:

MONDAY	TUESDAY	WEDNESDAY	THURSDAY
TO DO	TO DO	TO DO	TO DO
MEALS	MEALS	MEALS	MEALS

FRIDAY	SATURDAY	SUNDAY	NOTES
TO DO	TO DO	TO DO	
MEALS	MEALS	MEALS	MEALS

CRUISING TO DO LIST

CRUISE BUCKET LIST

PLACES I WANT TO VISIT:

THINGS I WANT TO SEE:

TOP 3 DESTINATIONS:

CRUISE ITINERARY

Monday

Tuesday

Wednesday

thursday

Friday

Saturday

Sunday

CRUISE OVERVIEW

MONTH:

MONDAY	TUESDAY	WEDNESDAY	THURSDAY	FRIDAY	SATURDAY	SUNDAY

CRUISE ACTIVITIES

WEEKLY ACTIVITY TRACKER: M T W T F S S

DAILY ACTIVITY PLANNER

DAILY ITINERARY

ACTIVITY: _____

TIME: _____

LOCATION: _____

WEATHER: ☀️ ⛅ 🌦️ ☁️ ⛈️

MEAL PLANNER

DAILY EXPENSES

TOTAL COST: [ ]

TOP ACTIVITIES

TIME: SCHEDULE:

NOTES:

CRUISE FRIENDS

FRIENDS ARE FOREVER

NAME:
PHONE NUMBER:
ADDRESS:
CABIN #:

FRIENDS ARE FOREVER

NAME:
PHONE NUMBER:
ADDRESS:
CABIN #:

FRIENDS ARE FOREVER

NAME:
PHONE NUMBER:
ADDRESS:
CABIN #:

FRIENDS ARE FOREVER

NAME:
PHONE NUMBER:
ADDRESS:
CABIN #:

There's Nothing Like Cruising Life!

CRUISE FRIENDS

FRIENDS ARE FOREVER

NAME:

PHONE NUMBER:

ADDRESS:

CABIN #:

FRIENDS ARE FOREVER

NAME:

PHONE NUMBER:

ADDRESS:

CABIN #:

FRIENDS ARE FOREVER

NAME:

PHONE NUMBER:

ADDRESS:

CABIN #:

FRIENDS ARE FOREVER

NAME:

PHONE NUMBER:

ADDRESS:

CABIN #:

There's Nothing Like Cruising Life!

CRUISE FRIENDS

FRIENDS ARE FOREVER

NAME:

PHONE NUMBER:

ADDRESS:

CABIN #:

FRIENDS ARE FOREVER

NAME:

PHONE NUMBER:

ADDRESS:

CABIN #:

FRIENDS ARE FOREVER

NAME:

PHONE NUMBER:

ADDRESS:

CABIN #:

FRIENDS ARE FOREVER

NAME:

PHONE NUMBER:

ADDRESS:

CABIN #:

There's Nothing Like Cruising Life!

CRUISE FRIENDS

FRIENDS ARE FOREVER

NAME:

PHONE NUMBER:

ADDRESS:

CABIN #:

FRIENDS ARE FOREVER

NAME:

PHONE NUMBER:

ADDRESS:

CABIN #:

FRIENDS ARE FOREVER

NAME:

PHONE NUMBER:

ADDRESS:

CABIN #:

FRIENDS ARE FOREVER

NAME:

PHONE NUMBER:

ADDRESS:

CABIN #:

There's Nothing Like Cruising Life!

CRUISE FRIENDS

FRIENDS ARE FOREVER

NAME:

PHONE NUMBER:

ADDRESS:

CABIN #:

FRIENDS ARE FOREVER

NAME:

PHONE NUMBER:

ADDRESS:

CABIN #:

FRIENDS ARE FOREVER

NAME:

PHONE NUMBER:

ADDRESS:

CABIN #:

FRIENDS ARE FOREVER

NAME:

PHONE NUMBER:

ADDRESS:

CABIN #:

There's Nothing Like Cruising Life!

CRUISE FRIENDS

FRIENDS ARE FOREVER

NAME:

PHONE NUMBER:

ADDRESS:

CABIN #:

FRIENDS ARE FOREVER

NAME:

PHONE NUMBER:

ADDRESS:

CABIN #:

FRIENDS ARE FOREVER

NAME:

PHONE NUMBER:

ADDRESS:

CABIN #:

FRIENDS ARE FOREVER

NAME:

PHONE NUMBER:

ADDRESS:

CABIN #:

There's Nothing Like Cruising Life!

MY CRUISE AGENDA

MY CRUISE AGENDA

MY CRUISE AGENDA

MY CRUISE AGENDA

MY CRUISE JOURNAL

DATE:

What I Did Today:

Highlight of the Day:

Thoughts & Reflections:

CRUISE SAVINGS

WE'RE SAVING FOR: _____

AMOUNT NEEDED: _____ $

OUR GOAL DATE: _____

DEPOSIT TRACKER

AMOUNT DEPOSITED: **DATE DEPOSITED:**

$ _____

$ _____

$ _____

$ _____

$ _____

$ _____

$ _____

$ _____

$ _____

$ _____

CRUISE SAVINGS

DEPOSIT TRACKER

AMOUNT DEPOSITED: **DATE DEPOSITED:**

$ _____ _____

$ _____ _____

$ _____ _____

$ _____ _____

$ _____ _____

$ _____ _____

$ _____ _____

$ _____ _____

$ _____ _____

$ _____ _____

$ _____ _____

$ _____ _____

$ _____ _____

CRUISE DETAILS

NOTES

TO DO:

CRUISE DETAILS & REMINDERS:

CRUISE COUNTDOWN

MONTH: _____ **YEAR:** _____

M	T	W	T	F	S	S

FLIGHT INFORMATION

DATE:	DESTINATION:

AIRLINE:	
BOOKING NUMBER:	
DEPARTURE DATE:	
BOARDING TIME:	
GATE NUMBER:	
SEAT NUMBER:	
ARRIVAL / LANDING TIME:	

DATE:	DESTINATION:

AIRLINE:	
BOOKING NUMBER:	
DEPARTURE DATE:	
BOARDING TIME:	
GATE NUMBER:	
SEAT NUMBER:	
ARRIVAL / LANDING TIME:	

CRUISE PACKING CHECKLIST

CLOTHING	✓	ESSENTIALS	✓

CRUISE PACKING CHECKLIST

CLOTHING FOR HER	✓	CLOTHING FOR HIM	✓

ESSENTIALS	✓	FOR THE JOURNEY	✓

		IMPORTANT DOCUMENTS	✓

CRUISE PACKING CHECKLIST

CLOTHING FOR HER	✓	CLOTHING FOR HIM	✓
T-Shirts &, Tank Tops & Blouses		T-Shirts & Tank Tops	
Sundresses		Shorts	
Flip Flops, Sandals & Heels		Swim Wear	
Shorts & Pants		Jeans, Khakis	
Swimsuit & Cover Up		Formal Attire (dress shirt, shoes, etc.)	
T-Shirts &, Tank Tops & Blouses		Belt	
Aqua/Swimming Shoes		Tie	
Bras, Panties & Socks		Sandals / Sneakers	
Sunhat		Visor, Baseball Cap	
Sunglasses		T-Shirts &, Tank Tops & Blouses	
Formal Attire		Sunglasses	
Jewelry		Socks & Underwear	

ESSENTIALS	✓	FOR THE JOURNEY	✓
Lanyard		Carry On Bag	
Suntan Lotion		Cash / Local Currency	
Medication (motion sickness, etc.)		Credit Cards	
Travel Mug / Water Bottle		Phone Charger	
		Backpack	

		IMPORTANT DOCUMENTS	✓
		Passport & ID	
		Cruise Documents & Boarding Pass	
		Flight Information	

CRUISE EXCURSION PLANNER

ACTIVITY / EXCURSION OVERVIEW:

EST COST OF EXCURSION:

INCLUSIONS: ✓

FOOD & DRINK: ☐

TRANSPORTATION: ☐

GRATUITY: ☐

EXCLUSIONS: ✓

☐

☐

☐

ACTUAL COST:

IMPORTANT INFORMATION:

CONTACT: _____ PHONE #: _____

MEET UP TIME: _____ WHAT TO BRING: _____

ADDRESS: _____

CRUISE PORT PLANNER

DESTINATION: **DATE:**

THINGS TO DO / SEE:

WHERE TO EAT:

TRANSPORTATION DETAILS:

OTHER INFORMATION:

RETURN TO SHIP BY:

ALL ABOARD!

PRE-CRUISE TO DO LIST & CHECKLIST

1 MONTH BEFORE

2 WEEKS BEFORE

1 WEEK BEFORE

2 DAYS BEFORE

24 HOURS BEFORE

DAY OF TRAVEL

CRUISE PLANNER

WEEK OF:

	MONDAY	TUESDAY	WEDNESDAY	THURSDAY
	TO DO	TO DO	TO DO	TO DO
	MEALS	MEALS	MEALS	MEALS

	FRIDAY	SATURDAY	SUNDAY	NOTES
	TO DO	TO DO	TO DO	
	MEALS	MEALS	MEALS	MEALS

CRUISING TO DO LIST

CRUISE BUCKET LIST

PLACES I WANT TO VISIT:

THINGS I WANT TO SEE:

TOP 3 DESTINATIONS:

CRUISE ITINERARY

Monday

Tuesday

Wednesday

thursday

Friday

Saturday

Sunday

CRUISE OVERVIEW

MONTH:

MONDAY	TUESDAY	WEDNESDAY	THURSDAY	FRIDAY	SATURDAY	SUNDAY

CRUISE ACTIVITIES

WEEKLY ACTIVITY TRACKER: M   T   W   T   F   S   S

DAILY ACTIVITY PLANNER

DAILY ITINERARY

ACTIVITY:
TIME:
LOCATION:
WEATHER:

MEAL PLANNER

DAILY EXPENSES

TOTAL COST:

TOP ACTIVITIES

TIME: SCHEDULE:

NOTES:

CRUISE FRIENDS

FRIENDS ARE FOREVER

NAME:

PHONE NUMBER:

ADDRESS:

CABIN #:

FRIENDS ARE FOREVER

NAME:

PHONE NUMBER:

ADDRESS:

CABIN #:

FRIENDS ARE FOREVER

NAME:

PHONE NUMBER:

ADDRESS:

CABIN #:

FRIENDS ARE FOREVER

NAME:

PHONE NUMBER:

ADDRESS:

CABIN #:

There's Nothing Like Cruising Life!

CRUISE FRIENDS

FRIENDS ARE FOREVER

NAME:

PHONE NUMBER:

ADDRESS:

CABIN #:

FRIENDS ARE FOREVER

NAME:

PHONE NUMBER:

ADDRESS:

CABIN #:

FRIENDS ARE FOREVER

NAME:

PHONE NUMBER:

ADDRESS:

CABIN #:

FRIENDS ARE FOREVER

NAME:

PHONE NUMBER:

ADDRESS:

CABIN #:

There's Nothing Like Cruising Life!

CRUISE FRIENDS

FRIENDS ARE FOREVER

NAME:

PHONE NUMBER:

ADDRESS:

CABIN #:

FRIENDS ARE FOREVER

NAME:

PHONE NUMBER:

ADDRESS:

CABIN #:

FRIENDS ARE FOREVER

NAME:

PHONE NUMBER:

ADDRESS:

CABIN #:

FRIENDS ARE FOREVER

NAME:

PHONE NUMBER:

ADDRESS:

CABIN #:

There's Nothing Like Cruising Life!

CRUISE FRIENDS

FRIENDS ARE FOREVER

NAME:
PHONE NUMBER:
ADDRESS:
CABIN #:

FRIENDS ARE FOREVER

NAME:
PHONE NUMBER:
ADDRESS:
CABIN #:

FRIENDS ARE FOREVER

NAME:
PHONE NUMBER:
ADDRESS:
CABIN #:

FRIENDS ARE FOREVER

NAME:
PHONE NUMBER:
ADDRESS:
CABIN #:

There's Nothing Like Cruising Life!

CRUISE FRIENDS

FRIENDS ARE FOREVER

NAME:

PHONE NUMBER:

ADDRESS:

CABIN #:

FRIENDS ARE FOREVER

NAME:

PHONE NUMBER:

ADDRESS:

CABIN #:

FRIENDS ARE FOREVER

NAME:

PHONE NUMBER:

ADDRESS:

CABIN #:

FRIENDS ARE FOREVER

NAME:

PHONE NUMBER:

ADDRESS:

CABIN #:

There's Nothing Like Cruising Life!

CRUISE FRIENDS

FRIENDS ARE FOREVER

NAME:

PHONE NUMBER:

ADDRESS:

CABIN #:

FRIENDS ARE FOREVER

NAME:

PHONE NUMBER:

ADDRESS:

CABIN #:

FRIENDS ARE FOREVER

NAME:

PHONE NUMBER:

ADDRESS:

CABIN #:

FRIENDS ARE FOREVER

NAME:

PHONE NUMBER:

ADDRESS:

CABIN #:

There's Nothing Like Cruising Life!

MY CRUISE AGENDA

MY CRUISE AGENDA

MY CRUISE AGENDA

MY CRUISE AGENDA

MY CRUISE JOURNAL

DATE:

What I Did Today:

Highlight of the Day:

Thoughts & Reflections:

CRUISE SAVINGS

WE'RE SAVING FOR:

AMOUNT NEEDED:

OUR GOAL DATE:

$

DEPOSIT TRACKER

AMOUNT DEPOSITED: **DATE DEPOSITED:**

$
$
$
$
$
$
$
$
$

CRUISE SAVINGS

DEPOSIT TRACKER

AMOUNT DEPOSITED: **DATE DEPOSITED:**

$ _____   _____

$ _____   _____

$ _____   _____

$ _____   _____

$ _____   _____

$ _____   _____

$ _____   _____

$ _____   _____

$ _____   _____

$ _____   _____

$ _____   _____

$ _____   _____

$ _____   _____

CRUISE DETAILS

NOTES

TO DO:

CRUISE DETAILS & REMINDERS:

CRUISE COUNTDOWN

MONTH: _____   **YEAR:** _____

M	T	W	T	F	S	S

FLIGHT INFORMATION

DATE: _____ DESTINATION: _____

AIRLINE:	
BOOKING NUMBER:	
DEPARTURE DATE:	
BOARDING TIME:	
GATE NUMBER:	
SEAT NUMBER:	
ARRIVAL / LANDING TIME:	

DATE: _____ DESTINATION: _____

AIRLINE:	
BOOKING NUMBER:	
DEPARTURE DATE:	
BOARDING TIME:	
GATE NUMBER:	
SEAT NUMBER:	
ARRIVAL / LANDING TIME:	

CRUISE PACKING CHECKLIST

CLOTHING	✓	ESSENTIALS	✓

CRUISE PACKING CHECKLIST

CLOTHING FOR HER	✓	CLOTHING FOR HIM	✓

ESSENTIALS	✓	FOR THE JOURNEY	✓

		IMPORTANT DOCUMENTS	✓

CRUISE PACKING CHECKLIST

CLOTHING FOR HER	✓	CLOTHING FOR HIM	✓
T-Shirts &, Tank Tops & Blouses		T-Shirts & Tank Tops	
Sundresses		Shorts	
Flip Flops, Sandals & Heels		Swim Wear	
Shorts & Pants		Jeans, Khakis	
Swimsuit & Cover Up		Formal Attire (dress shirt, shoes, etc.)	
T-Shirts &, Tank Tops & Blouses		Belt	
Aqua/Swimming Shoes		Tie	
Bras, Panties & Socks		Sandals / Sneakers	
Sunhat		Visor, Baseball Cap	
Sunglasses		T-Shirts &, Tank Tops & Blouses	
Formal Attire		Sunglasses	
Jewelry		Socks & Underwear	

ESSENTIALS	✓	FOR THE JOURNEY	✓
Lanyard		Carry On Bag	
Suntan Lotion		Cash / Local Currency	
Medication (motion sickness, etc.)		Credit Cards	
Travel Mug / Water Bottle		Phone Charger	
		Backpack	

IMPORTANT DOCUMENTS	✓
Passport & ID	
Cruise Documents & Boarding Pass	
Flight Information	

www.ingramcontent.com/pod-product-compliance
Lightning Source LLC
Chambersburg PA
CBHW081156070526
44583CB00021B/2868